Animal Bedtime

Jennifer Bové

Learn about the places animals choose to go to sleep.

Published by the National Wildlife Federation.

Photos provided by iStock.com:
Front Cover: John Carnernolla; Page 2: Schaef1; Page 4: Peter ten Broecke; Page 7: Charlie Miller KB; Page 8: moisseyev; Page 9: Peeraphont; Page 11: Thomas Lehtinen; Page 12: epantha; Page 13: Terryfic3D; Page 14: Tihis; Page 16: mildhightraveler; Page 17: krithnarong; Page 18: 400tmax; Page 19: TommL; Page 20: Hal Brindley; Page 22: Satit Srihin; Page 23: asxsoonxas; Page 24: ivz; Page 26: Ken Canning; Page 27: kugelblitz; Page 28: Prig-Studio; Page 29: SWKrull Imaging.

Additional Photos:
Page 5: Theodore Mattas.

Printed in the United States of America.

RangerRick.org

ISBN: 978-1-947254-35-0

Contents

Yawn! This fox is sleepy.

Animals get tired,
just like people do.
But animals don't
sleep in beds.
Let's find out where
animals like to doze.

A leopard lounges on a limb.

A sleeping sloth hangs from a branch.

A koala is cozy in
the crook of a tree.

A bear snoozes
on a bed of moss.

These fawns fell asleep in a grassy field and on a gravel path.

A hedgehog curls up tight to sleep.

River otters cuddle for a nap.

A meerkat family cuddles close together at bedtime.

Walruses pile up
on the seashore
to snore.

Bats sleep hanging upside down.

A polar bear doesn't mind the cold. It curls up in the snow for a nap.

Sea otters float
while fast asleep.

Mountain goats rest on a rocky ledge. Does that look comfy to you?

Author: JENNIFER BOVÉ

Question: If you were an animal, what would be your favorite kind of home?

Answer: I would not choose a tree branch (I might fall off). I would not choose a rocky ledge (it would be too hard). But, I would be perfectly comfy sleeping on a soft bed of moss like the bear in this book.

National Wildlife Federation Naturalist: DAVID MIZEJEWSKI

Question: Have you ever spotted an animal sleeping in the wild?

Answer: It's easy to spot sleeping turtles in ponds in the summertime. They climb out of the water onto fallen logs to bask in the sun and also to take a nap.

Illustrator: PARKER JACOBS *(Ranger Rick & Ricky characters)*

Question: When you were a kid, did you ever stay up drawing past bedtime?

Answer: When I was a kid, I did stay up drawing past my bedtime. In fact, it's a thing that I occasionally do as an adult. I have ruined too many pajamas and bed sheets by falling asleep with a pen in my hand.